CE in AMSTERDAM

Lucia Wilson   Anne Bowes

Katie Eggington

Anne Bowes

Cedric the Bear Ventures

ii

ISBN: 9798871122839 (paperback)

Publisher: Cedric the Bear Ventures

Copyright © 2019
Lucia Wilson & Katie Eggington & Anne Bowes

Lucia Wilson and Anne Bowes reserve the right to be identified as the author and illustrator of the work.

Author: Lucia Wilson

Illustrations and cover design: Anne Bowes

Original designer / Originator of Cedric the physical bear: Katie Eggington, and owner of the copyright of Cedric the physical bear.

All rights reserved. No part of this book may be used or reproduced by any means, graphic, electronical, or mechanical, including photocopying, recording, taping, or by any information storage retrieval system without the written permission of the publisher except in the case of brief quotations embodied in critical articles and reviews.

iv

CHAPTER 1

"Welcome to Amsterdam, Cedric!"

"Thomas! How wonderful to see you!" cried Cedric the bear who began to give his friend his biggest bear hug, but then gently released him.

"I hope I didn't hurt you, Thomas. How are you?"

"Oh well, as you know, I have just had my cataract surgery, just on this eye," he said, pointing to the eyepatch over his right eye, "and I will have to see how this one recovers. Then, if it goes well, which I'm sure it will, I will have the same surgery on my left eye."

"And how well can you see right now, Thomas?" asked Cedric.

"Well, not brilliantly today but I can manage if I am very careful. It is so good of you to come and help me out, Cedric, you can be my guide-bear!"

They both laughed at this, especially as Thomas himself was a former guide-dog. Thomas is a golden retriever, one of the most popular breeds for guide dogs in the Netherlands. It was a sad irony that Thomas, who had assisted so many blind people, was now in need of assistance himself. Cedric could tell that Thomas was a little downhearted and he made a promise to himself to help his friend as much as he could and to cheer him up.

***

Back at Thomas's home, a perfect little houseboat on one of the many canals in Amsterdam, Thomas and Cedric talked about all the things that old friends talk about when they meet each other after a long time.

"Tomorrow, I was thinking that I could show you around Amsterdam, after all, you've never been here before. Would you like that?"

"Oh, yes, please, Thomas! If you feel up to it. I am so curious about Amsterdam, and I can already see from your charming home that Amsterdam is one of the prettiest places I have ever visited."

"Wonderful! I shall enjoy introducing you to my home city and don't worry, together we can manage."

3

CHAPTER 2

The next day, the bright winter sunshine had encouraged Cedric and Thomas to have their breakfast outside on the deck of the houseboat. It was quite warm as the houseboat had solar-powered outdoor heating. Thomas was drinking his coffee whilst Cedric enjoyed some marigold tea (he never travelled anywhere without his favourite marigold tea). It was a delightful scene; the water was gently moving and made a soft repeated clapping sound against the pretty green boat, and other houseboat owners called out *'Goedemorgen'* – which is Dutch for good morning - as they floated by.

"You really have such a lovely home, Thomas! And such a perfect spot. I think the sound of water is so soothing."

"Yes, Cedric, I am extremely lucky to live here. And you have a lovely home, too, don't you?"

"Yes, I am lucky, too, Thomas. It's important to be happy in your home, isn't it?"

***

"Now, Thomas, please tell me how you want me to help you today."

"Okay, well the best thing is if you let me hold your paw, Cedric, rather than you hold mine. I know

Amsterdam very well, obviously, but my vision is quite blurry in my left eye and my right eye is still recovering so don't feel shy to tell me the street names as we go and give me a warning of any obstacles. Oh, and I should tell you to watch out for the bikes!" said Thomas with a laugh.

"Amsterdam is famous for its cycle lanes, which are very practical and good for the environment because it means there are less cars and there is less pollution. That said, some of the cyclists are pretty fast, Cedric, and if you don't pay attention to the cycle lanes, you could easily have an accident. With this eye-patch and the blurry vision in my left eye, well, we both need to take extra care. Now let's head for the tram."

Sitting on the tram, Cedric was delighted by all the lovely buildings in different colours and the exciting way the cyclists crossed the city whilst navigating the many canals.

Soon they were walking over the bridge that led towards the famous Rijksmuseum, one of the finest museums in the world. Cedric gasped at the grand building set against a pale blue sky.

"It's so beautiful!" cried Cedric, "really impressive!"

"And just wait until you see what's inside, Cedric!" said Thomas with pride. He held onto Cedric's paw as they stepped inside the great museum. "I don't think we should try and see everything today, Cedric, it's far too big. Shall I take you to some of the main galleries for now?"

"Yes, please, Thomas, that would be perfect."

They set off to explore the museum and saw the stunning artworks of Rembrandt, Van Gogh, Vermeer and many more. Thomas also showed Cedric the amazing Delft ceramic objects which Cedric really admired.

"I love the colour blue with white, and what interesting and wonderful ceramic pieces, like this fantastic tulip vase and look at that violin," said Cedric with wide eyes.

"Now come with me, there's something else that I think you will love," and Thomas led the way to a darkened gallery with heavy curtains and window shutters: it felt like a church. When Cedric's eyes adjusted to the light, he saw an astonishing sight – the most beautiful dolls' houses!

They were wonderful replicas of elegant houses with the finest furniture, tiny yet perfect in every detail. Cedric couldn't take his eyes off them. He was so keen to look more closely that he bumped his head on the glass barrier that protected the dolls' houses. Cedric would have stayed there all day looking at them but there were so many people in the queue that Thomas had to pull his friend away.

"Marvellous, quite astonishing! There is something magical about them."

Thomas smiled at Cedric as if he had a secret to tell him, but then they heard the announcement that the Rijksmuseum would be closing in fifteen minutes, and everyone began to move towards the exits.

"Why are they closing so early?" asked Cedric.

"It's half-day opening today," said Thomas.

Cedric and Thomas were being swept along by the crowd when Thomas suddenly pulled Cedric into a small, curtained alcove. Cedric looked surprised but Thomas whispered, "wait."

Soon the galleries were empty as the security staff swiftly ushered the visitors out of the museum. Cedric was desperate to sneeze as they hid behind the dusty curtains but managed not to make any noise. He looked at Thomas with a puzzled expression. Eventually the rooms became dark except for the security lights and Cedric couldn't hear anything except his own breathing.

"Okay, we can come out now. I have a surprise for you. Come with me."

Thomas led Cedric back to the room with the dolls' houses. All was dark and still.

"Johannes, it's me, Thomas," said Thomas in a low voice.
Suddenly, as if a switch had been flipped, all the dolls' houses were flooded with light and burst into life, with tiny people moving about! Talking, eating, laughing, cooking, one person was playing a piano, another was singing beside him whilst children danced. Cedric could not believe his eyes! Thomas laughed to see his face.

"Thomas, how good to see you! And you've had your operation. How are you? And who is this with you?" called a smartly dressed man the size of a matchstick.

"Johannes, meet Cedric. Cedric, this is Johannes. He and I are old friends."

Cedric was still recovering from the shock and stumbled over his words. Thomas and Johannes laughed.

"Would you like to join us for some tea?" suggested Johannes with a cheeky expression.

Cedric looked even more confused. 'How on earth could they share tea together from their tiny cups?' he thought but didn't like to sound rude, so he said nothing.

Thomas smiled and said,

"Are you ready for an adventure, Cedric?"

"Oh, yes, always ready!"

"Okay, see that beam of sunlight coming through the shutters? Well, we need to stand right on that spot. Are you ready to bring us in, Johannes?"

"Ready!"

And they both stepped into the perfect circle of light on the museum floor.

"Hold onto me, Cedric!"

With a loud whirring sound, Cedric and Thomas began to spin. Cedric felt like he was on the fastest fairground ride in the world. It was thrilling! Faster and faster, they went, so fast that Cedric couldn't see anything, and he held on tight to Thomas.

Then just as suddenly, they were standing in front of Johannes. They were the same height as him!

Cedric was utterly speechless as Johannes shook his paw heartily.

"But.. what... I can't believe it!" cried Cedric with a laugh.

Johannes smiled and said, 'Sit down, please, and have some tea."

Johannes turned to Thomas and gave him a warm hug.

"Always good to see you, my dear friend. The saviour of the PHC, the Poppenhuizen Community," he added solemnly.

"Poppenhuizen means Dolls' Houses in Dutch, Cedric."

"Oh, thank you for explaining that" and turning to Thomas, Cedric whispered, "why did he call you 'the saviour of the PHC'?"

Thomas gave a shake of his tail as if slightly embarrassed and looked at Cedric. "I'll tell you later" he whispered, turning their attention to the delicious treats in front of them and drank tea from fine blue and white cups whilst Cedric looked around him in delight and wonder at the extraordinary experience.

As they talked, Thomas began to realise something was worrying Johannes.

"Johannes, what is it? I know you well, my friend, something is on your mind."

"Ah, I don't want to trouble you, Thomas, you've already done so much for us."

"Please tell me what it is."

"We are being evicted! Forced to move!"

"Oh no, what has happened, Johannes?"

"The museum wants to transfer us to New York, and we don't want to go!"

"Are you saying that you have spoken to Nina Boheemse, the director of the museum? Has she found out about you all?!" said Thomas looking shocked.

"No, no…" he turned to Cedric, "no one knows we are here, Cedric, only Thomas and Dr Elsa. Thomas has a special honorary status with us which is why he can be brought in, as you both were today.

Only I know the secret code to bring the Giants into the Community. We have lived here undisturbed for centuries. "

Turning back to Thomas he said, "we heard all of this when the Museum director was discussing her plans with the director from New York here in our room. We don't want to go to New York. This is our home!"

"What are you going to do?" said Thomas.

"I don't know!" said Johannes despairingly.

Cedric looked at Johannes and said,

"I think you may need a lawyer, Johannes."

"You are right, Cedric. However, that would involve revealing our community to the Giants and the outside world. It's a big risk. I don't think the Giants will understand us – present company excepted; no offence intended."

"None taken," said Thomas. "It would definitely be a big risk for you."

"Does anyone else know that you are here?" asked Cedric.

"Yes, Dr Elsa van Heusen. Thomas brought her to us when we had a deadly sickness spreading through the Community."

Thomas then explained, "Dr Elsa is the daughter of my last master, Cedric. I was his guide-dog. I brought her father here for a special tour that they arrange for blind people. Whilst he was on the tour, I was waiting here, and something set my dog senses tingling and I heard crying."

"Yes, it was the crying of one of my neighbours, she was distraught because her little girl was so sick," added Johannes. "So, I decided to trust Thomas – the first Giant that I have ever spoken to – and I told him about the mysterious disease that was making all the children ill.

Thomas then told me about Dr Elsa and what a clever and kind doctor she was, and that he would bring her to us if I agreed.

Of course, Dr Elsa was very confused about how she could treat the sick children until she understood about the secret code. As the elected head of the Poppenhuizen Community, I have the secret code and no one else. When I retire, I will pass it on. So, I brought in Dr Elsa, and she set to work with Thomas and myself as her assistants. Dr Elsa and Thomas worked tirelessly until all the children were saved.

Without Thomas, we would never have met Dr Elsa. I don't care to think about what would have happened to us all. Certainly, Dr Elsa will not give us away."

"And besides," added Thomas, "she is bound by patient confidentiality; doctors must never discuss their patients."

"So, other than Dr Elsa and Thomas, no one else in Amsterdam knows that you are here. You are quite safe for now, yes? Good, that means we have time to think of a plan to deal with this problem" said Cedric energetically.

"Yes, but there's not a lot of time, Cedric. We are going to be moved in less than a month. We must act fast."

***

22

CHAPTER 3

Unfortunately, the PHC (the Poppenhuizen Community) had another problem that they didn't even know about. On the other side of Amsterdam, Dr Erik van Heusen, Dr Elsa's twin brother – yes, he was also a doctor, but he was not a kind one - knew about the Poppenhuizen Community, as well. He had secretly followed his sister when she went with Thomas to help them during the 'mysterious sickness.' Ever since that time, evil Dr Erik had been looking for an opportunity to take advantage of the existence of the PHC. Dr Erik had also heard about the Rijksmuseum's plan to transfer the Dolls' Houses to New York; time was running out for him to benefit from this secret. He sat at home, brooding on a way to make his name, to be more famous than his twin sister, and he didn't care how he did it.

"I've got it!" he shouted and slapped the table in front of him. He began ringing every newspaper and online broadcaster he could to sell his story.

He hinted at a great scoop about a secret community of tiny talking dolls somewhere in Amsterdam, but they must all pay him a lot of money first. He also declared that he was claiming "Finders-Keepers" status, which was very sinister. Only after he reached his target of two million euros would he reveal the true location of this secret community.

Dr Erik really was a terrible man!

25

CHAPTER 4

A little later, Cedric and Thomas were studying several legal websites when Thomas caught something on the TV news.

"Oh, no! This is a disaster! Did you hear what the newsreader just said?"

"Sorry, Thomas, it's all Dutch to me!" said Cedric with a smile.

"Ha Ha! Of course, sorry, Cedric. You see the man speaking now, well that is the brother of Dr Elsa, it's Dr Erik van Heusen. He's her twin, her evil twin in fact! He is as bad as she is good."

"What's he done?"

"Somehow he has learned about the existence of the PHC! He must have followed Dr Elsa, or maybe he read the confidential patient notes – he's not saying how he knows, but he knows, Cedric!"

"Oh, no!" cried Cedric.

"He is being very sly; he is only telling the media a small bit of the information and he wants more money to give them the exact location of what he is describing as a 'secret community of tiny talking dolls in the heart of Amsterdam'! And he's claiming "Finders-Keepers" rights. Oh, he is so bad!"

Cedric was appalled.

"He can't do that! They are not talking dolls; they are small humans! How can he claim "Finders-Keepers" status? He's treating them as if they are just objects" said Cedric in an outraged voice.

"Absolutely. Now the pressure is on, Cedric. We have got to get top legal advice for the PHC straight away."

He picked up his phone and began to dial.

"Sir Eduard?" said Thomas. "This is Thomas, I need to see you urgently, please. Can I come there, with my friend, Cedric? Yes? Thank you. We'll come at once!"

Grabbing Cedric's paw, Thomas pulled him out of the door.

Thomas was in such a hurry that Cedric had no time to ask where they were going. They hailed a taxi and drove at top speed – to the zoo.

At the zoo, Thomas was following his nose rather than using his eyes and dropping down onto all fours he dashed on ahead, his tail swishing through the air. Cedric also had to get on all fours to keep up with him!

"That was quick, Thomas" called a voice from above.

Looking up, Cedric saw a beautiful Ransuil owl, a long-eared owl native to the Netherlands.

"Cedric, let me introduce you to Sir Eduard de Groot. One of the best lawyers in the whole of the Netherlands, no, the whole of Europe."

"Too kind, Thomas, always too kind," said the owl, with a voice so deep that it made the leaves tremble. Then, he spread his massive wings that momentarily blocked out the light as he flew above them and with a majestic swoop, he landed in front of Thomas and Cedric.

Sir Eduard opened a door in the bark of the tree and invited them to follow him. He reached for his barrister's gown and collar and put them on.

"So, to business. Give me the facts, Thomas."

Sitting behind his desk in his cluttered office at the base of the tree, Sir Eduard listened intently whilst his personal assistant, a short-eared owl known as a Velduil owl, Eva Reinhard, made copious notes on her laptop. Her owl's eyes looked even bigger behind her huge, black spectacles.

Turning to Eva, Sir Eduard spoke quickly in a quiet voice as she nodded in reply to his instructions. Cedric was overawed by the sense that a giant legal brain was at work.

Suddenly, Sir Eduard turned to Thomas and Cedric, his long ears quivering with energy, his intelligent eyes sharp and commanding and said firmly,

"Here is my advice: you must lodge a claim immediately at the Court of Justice and Fairness to establish protected status for the Poppenhuizen Community. Ms Reinhard, my para-legal – although I tend to call her my para-eagle as she is so sharp-eyed," he said with a low chuckle, "is going to prepare the document for you to take with you, firstly to the PHC, for their approval and signature. And then, with all speed, you must lodge the claim today."

"Oh, thank you Sir Eduard, but can I ask, how exactly will this help the PHC?" asked Thomas.

"Protected Status for the PHC means they are untouchable, and, most importantly, they cannot be moved without their agreement! But you must hurry, Thomas!"

***

In the meantime, Dr Erik was working on his own wicked plan of action.

***

As Thomas and Cedric returned to the Rijksmuseum at top speed, he received a call on his mobile. It was Dr Elsa van Heusen.

"Thomas, I am ringing you to warn you that my brother, Erik, is up to no good."

"Yes, we know! I saw him on the news!"

"I know that he has broken into my filing cabinet and taken the notes for the Poppenhuizen Community, which is a terrible thing to do. On top of which, I think he has also taken a special sedative gas from my medicine cabinet. Oh, he's planning something terrible. Our poor father would be so sad to see him behaving so badly. I think he's heading for the Museum!"

"So, are we, Dr Elsa, can you join us there, perhaps you can persuade him not to do whatever it is that he's planning? "

"I will come right away."

***

As they reached the Rijksmuseum, they found Dr Elsa near the entrance.

"We have a problem – I'm not sure how we can get back in, it's closed to the public now!" said Thomas with a worried expression.

"I know what we can do, follow me" said Dr Elsa. She presented her medical badge to the door attendant and spoke briskly.

"Medical emergency! I'm Dr van Heusen, these are my colleagues" and she marched straight passed the guard without waiting for him to answer with Thomas and Cedric following behind her. Cedric and Thomas were very impressed. They rushed on to the gallery with the dolls' houses.

"Johannes, it's Thomas. We must be quick. I have Dr Elsa and Cedric with me. You need to bring us in straightaway," and all three of them stood below the late afternoon sunlight, waiting. Moments later they were all standing in front of Johannes, as Thomas explained the situation.

"So, you see, Johannes, you must sign these papers now and we will take them to the Court of Justice and Fairness immediately. It closes at 6.30pm so we must hurry."

As Johannes signed the papers, Thomas's dog senses began to tingle. Something was wrong, there was a bad presence.

He was sure they were being watched. Suddenly, strange smoke appeared. It was gas! It was sedative gas! Who could have done such a thing?

"Oh, Erik! What have you done?" said Dr Elsa as she saw her brother's face. Then she collapsed onto the floor, followed by Johannes and Thomas. Cedric, however, had quickly covered his snout with a tea towel and hid himself behind a large screen. He could see Dr Erik talking to himself about his Finders-Keepers claim.

"Hah! Now I've won. They'll never make it to the court in time!" He swiftly turned on his heels and rushed away.

Cedric realised he had to get the signed PHC document to the Court of Justice and Fairness.

"But how can I get back to full size?" he asked himself. "Johannes is unconscious and he's the only person who knows the code!" Suddenly a voice behind him said quietly,

"Don't worry, I know the code."

Cedric jumped.

"Who's there?" said Cedric, confused and frightened.

He slowly turned around, peering into a darkened corner.

"I'm Johannes's shadow, I know the code. I can help you get back so that you can save us all."

"Oh, that's...that's brilliant!" said Cedric, much relieved. "Please hurry and send me back to full size," as he grabbed the signed document. "But wait, what about the others? They are still unconscious. Will they be okay?"

"Let me take care of them. I will speak to Dr Rutte who joined our community recently. Hurry, get ready, I am going to send you back!"

Soon, Cedric was dashing from the Museum. He was about to jump into a taxi but then he realised that it was the height of the rush hour, and the traffic was barely moving. He knew that the courthouse would close at 6.30pm and Sir Eduard was insistent that the claim had to be lodged today.

"Oh, no, oh, no. I would be quicker to run, but I don't know the way." He decided to call Sir Eduard. Eva answered. He explained his dilemma.

"Leave it with me, Cedric, stay right there," she said efficiently and hung up.

As he stood on the pavement, Cedric waited impatiently, hopping from one paw to the other, not really knowing what would happen next. Suddenly, he saw the magnificent sight of the giant, outstretched wings of Sir Eduard swooping down towards him then hovering in the air.

"Quickly, Cedric, hand me the papers!"

"Here Sir, thank you Eduard, Sir! I mean, Sir Eduard!"

And with a mighty whoosh, Sir Eduard was gone.

'I hope he makes it in time' thought Cedric anxiously.

43

CHAPTER 5

The following morning, Dr Erik was in a small square near to the Rijksmuseum. A group of reporters, camera operators and photographers were jostling together taking photographs and firing questions.

"All in good time, ladies, and gentlemen, all in good time. I promised you a great surprise and, I assure you, you will not be disappointed."

He scoured the crowd and felt very pleased with himself until he spotted one face, that of his sister, Dr Elsa. She had returned to full size with the help of Johannes's shadow and Dr Rutte.

Dr Elsa didn't speak but just looked straight into his eyes with a very sad expression. Deciding to ignore her, Dr Erik called to the crowd,

"Follow me!"

As he passed Elsa, she grabbed his sleeve and said, "Do you think our father would be proud of you today, Erik? Please think about what harm you are causing. Not just to the Poppenhuizen Community, but to yourself – and to me."

For a moment, Dr Erik hesitated, and a look of confusion crossed his face. Then, he pushed his sister away and walked on with a trail of people bustling after him.

***

Back at the PHC, Thomas was also back to full size, with Cedric beside him. Johannes had recovered as well but was waiting anxiously to know their fate. No-one had heard yet from Sir Eduard, but suddenly there was a great swarm of people moving towards the Dolls Houses, as more and more people attached themselves to the crowd that followed Dr Erik. Thomas barked loudly, trying, in vain, to stop them, but he knew it was hopeless.

Theatrically, Dr Erik turned around, raised his hand, and told the crowd to stop where they were. He was enjoying his powerful position immensely.

"I told you that I have discovered a secret community of tiny talking dolls, and here they are!"

Then he faced Thomas and said,

"Stand aside, Thomas! And you" he said to Cedric. "Who are you anyway?"

"I'm Cedric the Bear, Thomas's friend" said Cedric proudly, "and you are a very wicked man."

Dr Elsa who was now standing beside Cedric in front of the dolls' houses turned to whisper to Johannes,

"Hide, Johannes, hurry."

"No," he said, "I think, Dr Elsa, it's time for us to stop hiding, it's time to stop being afraid of the Giants."

And one by one all the Poppenhuizen Community came out of their hiding places and stood proudly with Johannes. For a moment everyone in the museum was silent, shocked by the amazing sight.

Then, Dr Erik drew out a document from his pocket and shouted

"Finders-Keepers! I claim ownership of these talking dolls!"

"We are not talking dolls; we are just like you! We are humans, we are just smaller than you" declared Johannes. "You can't own us!"

And before Dr Erik could reply, with a mighty rush of air that made everyone lean backwards, Sir Eduard and Ms Eva Reinhard flew in through the window.

Johannes smiled broadly.

"And besides, we have Protected Status! You cannot touch us, you can't own us, and…" turning to the Museum director, he said, "*you* cannot move us. We don't want to go to New York, and you can't force us to go. This is our home."

There was a lot of noise and questions and then, with a voice that made everyone's hair fly up and tremble, Sir Eduard declared,

"It is all in order. I lodged the papers myself yesterday.

And you, Dr Erik, you should be ashamed of yourself for thinking you could ever own another human being. It is a criminal offence. The Finders-Keepers rule is for objects, only, not people! I believe, those gentlemen over there are waiting to speak with you, Dr Erik," and he pointed one wing in the direction of the police officers just behind the crowd. The police officers came forward and took Dr Erik away.

Dr Elsa looked at Thomas, and in a sad, quiet voice said,

"I... I have to.. he has behaved very badly, but .."

"I know," said Thomas gently, "he is still your brother. You go, we understand."

Meanwhile, the Museum Director, Nina Boheemse, turned to Johannes and said, "well, we have a lot to discuss, and perhaps, Sir Eduard, you might wish to sit in on our meeting so that you can see that all is in good legal order, fair and just? And that the rights of the PHC are respected?"

"Yes, of course, it would be my pleasure, and my paralegal, Ms. Eva Reinhard, will take notes."

A great cheer rose up from the Poppenhuizen Community and everyone hugged each other and laughed.

"Thank you, Thomas! And thank you, Cedric!" said Johannes. "We couldn't have done it without you all!"

"Graag gedaan!" said Thomas.

"You're welcome!" added Cedric.

THE CEDRIC TEAM

Cedric the bear is the original creation of Katie Eggington. Both Cedric and Katie were featured in the BBC programme, Paul Martin's Handmade Revolution in 2012. Katie was one of the winning designers and Cedric was proudly displayed in the V&A Museum shop.

On seeing the programme, Lucia Wilson decided to approach Katie to discuss creating a series of children's stories based on Cedric. Anne Bowes (a talented illustrator and jewellery designer) joined the project and has created some delightful illustrations. Lucia, Katie, and Anne worked together to bring Cedric to life in the first book, with three stories, which is called The Adventures of Cedric the Bear.

Katie Eggington – Original Creator of Cedric

Katie Eggington is the designer and creative force behind Creative Threads. Having graduated from Norwich University for the Arts with a first-class BA (Hons) degree in Woven Textiles, Katie carved out a unique product in her distinctive handmade, woven teddy bears. Working from her home studio in Hampshire, Katie meticulously designs and brings to life each bear individually. Cedric was featured in the BBC series, Paul Martin's Handmade Revolution. As a winner, Cedric was displayed at the Victoria and Albert Museum, London. Katie's wider collection of work has also earned its place in the media spotlight, with features in publications including the Dorset Echo, Eastern Daily Press, and the NUA Alumni Magazine. Katie now shares her wealth of weave experience and knowledge with the next generation through her technical weave blog Creative Threads: creative-threads.co.uk

Lucia Wilson - Author of the Cedric stories
Lucia Wilson is a British-born Anglo-Burmese writer of poetry, lyrics, and stories for all ages. She is a member of SACEM and PRS and lives in London. Lucia's novella, The Karloff Tiara, is available on Amazon. In the summer of 2016, Lucia decided to ask Katie if she would like to collaborate on a series of children's books about Cedric and this led to the creation of *Cedric at the Museum*, *Cedric and the Button Bear* and *Cedric in Paris* with illustrations by Anne Bowes. Details of other books by Lucia can be found at www.luciawilson.co.uk

Anne Bowes – Illustrator of the Cedric book
Anne Bowes is an illustrator and jewellery designer based in London. She studied Decorative Arts and Textiles at Camberwell School of Art before going onto a career in graphic design and illustration. Anne studied Jewellery design in Hatton Garden and created her jewellery brand Anne Bowes Jewellery in 2010.

Instagram AnneBowesIllustration
www.annebowesillustration.com
annebowesjewellery.com
Instagram AnneBowesJewellery

For more information and more Cedric stories, please visit:

 www.cedricthebear.com

Do you like owls?

We do! During the creation of this book, I did some research about owls native to the Netherlands and contacted the Royal Society for the Protection of Birds, the RSPB in the UK. A very helpful young woman called Sian suggested that I should contact Vogelbescherming in the Netherlands to find out more about owls in the Netherlands.

I wrote to Vogelbescherming, and I met (via email, of course) another very helpful young woman by the name of Eva who was good enough not only to tell me the Dutch names of the owls native to the Netherlands, but also sent us some reference material to help us, and it certainly did.

Creating this book has made us so curious to learn more about owls and other birds!

If you would like to know more about our feathered friends, you should visit the fantastic websites of www.vogelbescherming.nl and www.rspb.org.uk .

Warmest wishes,

Lucia, Anne, Katie (and Cedric!)

Printed in Great Britain
by Amazon

47050238R00036